THE EPIC OF INDIAN WOMANHOOD

THE EPIC OF INDIAN WOMANHOOD

K. S. RAMASWAMI SASTRI

GYAN

Published by

GYAN

Gyan Publishing House
5, Ansari Road
Daryaganj, New Delhi-110002
Phone: 011-47034999, 9811692060
E-mail: books@gyanbooks.com

Distribution Network
gyanbooks.com
India, USA, Canada, UK, Australia

ISBN: 978-93-6920-055-9 (PB)

First Published, 1921

2nd Impression 2025

Printed at: Gyan Press, Delhi.

THE EPIC OF INDIAN WOMANHOOD
Author: K. S. RAMASWAMI SASTRI

THE EPIC OF INDIAN WOMANHOOD

THE EPIC OF INDIAN WOMANHOOD

BY

K. S. RAMASWAMY SASTRY, B.A., B.L.

WITH AN INTRODUCTION BY

Dr. RADHAKUMUD MOOKERJI, M.A., Ph.D.,
University Professor, Mysore.

THE IMPERIAL TRADING CO.,
TRIPLICANE, - - - MADRAS, S. E.

SOLDEN & CO., MADRAS, S.E.

CONTENTS

INTRODUCTION

I feel honoured by the request of Mr. K. S. Rama swamy Sastry B.A., B.L., that I should introduce to the public his new work in verse, *The Epic of Indian Womanhood.* It is a real pleasure to me to have thus an opportunity of associating myself with one for whom I have come to entertain a great regard not merely for his many and varied writings to which the literary world is regularly treated, but for the type of training and mind they represent. We find in him a rare example of a love of art or culture for its own sake that refuses to be extinguished in the uncongenial atmosphere of his official life. It is like a spring which has in secret attained to such hidden heights that, in spite of the lower levels, the solid, and arid, strata, through which it has to course in its career, it is not lost, but is carried along by its own momentum, until it emerges into view as a shooting fountain of beauty and strength! What in him has further struck me is the cast of his mind with its genuinely Hindu and national bent that no amount of modern culture can ever twist, or deflect from its native and original inclination. It is to such minds that Hindu India confidently looks for the interpretation and justification of her culture to the world. Such a mission Mr. Ramaswamy Sastry has been throughout serving; and the present work is the latest proof of it. An Indian's attempt at composition of English poetry is, however, liable to be misunderstood and is, in some senses, hard to be justified. But there is a point of view from which such an attempt may be condoned, nay, welcomed. Under present conditions of education, the youth of India are nurtured upon English poetry as part of the curriculum of the schools, and advantage may well be taken of this feature in their studies to introduce to them such English poetry as is English only in its garb, but Indian in its contents or substance. Thus one more step may be taken towards nationalising our system of education that is derived so largely from alien inspiration and models and directed so dominantly by alien agencies. If we are asked to define what we exactly mean by this criticism, the reply is that our education thus inspired and directed necessarily fails at every step and stage to adjust itself to the true needs and requirements of the nation, of which the most glaring instance is the introduction of our youths to literature which tells of a life and an environment absolutely foreign to their experience, and thus loses a large part of its educative value. Most of the studies prescribed for our young students thus become unduly abstract in their character to which they cannot completely respond. We are not, of course, to taboo English literature, but we should taboo such of its specimens as are more English than human in their contents or composition, more local than universal in their appeal, when they are intended especially for tender minds. As an example of English literature breathing Indian atmosphere and giving expression to Indian sentiments and ideals *The Epic of Indian Womanhood* will be a welcome substitute for works to be eliminated from the curriculum of our schools on the pedagogic principle stated above. The book is the fruit of a happy wedding of English language, free from flaws, and Indian ideas at their best. We hope it is only the first instalment of a series on a subject which can hardly be exhausted.

Mysore University,
Mysore.
January 1921.

RADHAKUMUD MOOKERJI.

THE EPIC OF INDIAN WOMANHOOD.

SAKUNTALA

SING, Muse, of her who showed to all the world
The raptures of devoted love, and won
By her dispassion and her purity
A higher bliss than passion could bestow.
In Kanwa's hermitage she grew in light
Of loveliness and purity of soul.
Descended from the nymph of heaven what time
She drew with beauty's charm the mighty sage
Who self-subdued in penance sat of yore,
Sakuntala in Kanwa's *Ashram* lived
As his pet foster-child. Her playmates fair,
Priyamvada and Anasuya good,
Made forest life a feast of pure delights.
They tended flowering creepers, plants, and trees
Till all the *Ashram* laughed with varied bloom.
The fawns with large and lustrous tender eyes
Which matched her eyes in witching loveliness
Her golden lotus feet played glad around.
Thus grew in beauty fair Sakuntala

Amidst the purest, sweetest nature's sights,
And her fair frame to beauty's fulness rose
As crescent rounds to full moon's argent orb
In sapphire skies.
                    One radiant summer morn
Dushyanta, king of that fair holy land
And born in Puru's great imperial line,
With huntsmen hunting went by Fate's behest.
On sport intent he came to save his land [men
From prowling beasts that harmed the peaceful
And tillèd fields. His chariot flew with speed
But quicker than it fled a startled fawn
With shrinking limbs which feared the royal shafts,
And oft-turned face that cast its trembling looks
At his pursuing car, and flying feet
That seemed to leap on air and earth disdain.
The chariot sped full fast behind the deer.
The arrow swift was fitted to the bow,
But ere it was on deadly errand loosed,
A gentle but imperious voice in tones
Of pleading cried: " Thy keen and deadly shafts
Like wingéd lightning swift must never fail
On such a gentle creature as this deer.
The royal power is given by mighty God
To punish ill and not to hurt the pure."
The king in haste laid by his well-bent bow

And made obeisance meet to him who spoke
In gentle tones of pleading for the fawn.
And at the hermit's request went the king
To Kanwa's *Ashram* fair to rest awhile.
And as he went he saw the blossomed trees
Bear luscious fruits and give sweet restful shade.
A holy calm did brood o'er all the place
And brought the joys of peace to human hearts.
And rival creatures that deep hatred bore
Forgot their hate and felt the force of love
That came with unseen might from saintly souls.
The sweet-toned voices of three maidens fair
Fell like a gentle shower of melody
Upon the royal ears. He stepped behind
A lofty tree and saw a wondrous sight.
A maiden with the crown of perfect youth
And sceptred with resplendent loveliness
Ruled all that fair domain of gentle peace
With shining eyes and face and sainted heart.
The golden sunbeams that around her played
An added glory seemed to draw from her
Bright golden frame. The fair surrounding flowers
Did seem to bend to touch with yearning love
The lotus of her perfect face. The fawns
With large eyes fixed upon her starlike eyes

Her followed with their sweet and trustful love.
She and her playmates fair with pitchers full
Upon their hips enrobed in barks of trees
The plants with water fed. The creepers fair
With eager thirst for nectar of her looks
And not for water laughed with joy in flowers
When came near them the fair Sakuntala.
The king's right arm then felt a fateful throb.
He saw how bright she was though dressed in barks.
The forest bloom outshone the garden flowers
That in the palace shone. The lotus flower
Is fair despite the green surrounding moss.
The spot of darkness in the shining moon
Adds but new beauty to its silver shield.
Then near and nearer came the maidens fair
As full moon followed by two silver stars.
With rich red lips that pouted sweet, and arms
That shone like flowering creepers fair, and youth
That stole the senses like a fragrant bloom,
She came with regnant grace and loveliness.
She saw her favourite creeper named by her
The light of all the bower! The mango tree
That stood by its bright side its sweet embrace
Received with joy and thrilled with tender leaves

Where sang the *Kokila* with love's sweet notes.
The king's pure heart for her love's heavenly grace
With yearning prayed.
While thus in rapture stood
The king, an amorous bee there flying came
And buzzed around her shining lotus face.
Like happy lover, it her glances coy
Received and seemed to whisper in her ears.
Again and yet again her lips it sought.
She cried for help and at this came in view
The king to save her from th' intruding bee.
Their glances mingled and a sudden love
Shone in their hearts with quick and heavenlit [flame.
But when he sought her bright and sweet converse
She could not speak from shyness, though her eyes
His goodly person sought with lovelooks fair
That oft returned as oft he turned away.
He learnt from her companions dear the tale
Of her bright heavenly birth and soothed his heart
As she who seemed above his kingly reach
Was fit his throne to grace. What seemed to him
A spark of fire was but a ruby bright.
Sakuntala then rose to go away
With shyness overcome ; but her dear friend
Priyamvada forbade as she a debt

To her must pay, as she two tender trees
Had watered on her friend's behalf. The king
Unwilling that his heart's glad-chosen Queen
Should do such work then said : " This lady fair
Is weary with the work ; her shoulders droop ;
Her tender palms blush with unfitting toil ;
Her bosom trembles with deep-taken breath ;
The flower that decks her ear hangs drooping there ;
Her flowing tresses held by tender hand
Dishevelled shine behind her full-moon face ;
Let me her debt most gladly pay." Her friend
Declared her free from debt at this. But yet
Sakuntala did linger there in love.
The ring that great Dushyanta gave as pledge
Of his desire to pay her debt disclosed
His lineage high and his imperial rank.
And as the sunset's bright far-shining hues
The west made like a wondrous paradise
The maidens homeward went. Sakuntala
As though a thorn had pricked her stayed and [turned
To see the gazing king, and yet again
She stayed as though a branch had caught her [dress
And round the neck of her belovéd king

The garland of her glances threw with joy.
The king went with a forward-moving frame
And backward-moving heart that sought the maid·
And as he reached his camp, the full-orbed moon
O'er all the world her sweet enchantments threw.
The love-lorn king was lost in thoughts of her
Whose moon-bright face lit his heart's paradise.
When morn returned and with her fingers drew
Night's curtains dark and led the bridegroom sun
In sight of all the world, the king resolved
To send his men to town and stay behind
To live in light of his fair lady's eyes.
The sages in the Ashram prayed his stay
And this was joy to him as he could see
The glory of his eyes and bliss of soul.
And as his wandering feet beside the stream
That sang through that reposeful hermitage
In languor went, he saw within a bower
Sakuntala upon a bed of flowers
Reposing ill at ease, and fanned by friends.
Her loveliness was more than e'er before,
But languor caused by love by her concealed
Had thinned her frame and made her wan and [pale.
With shyness overcome she slowly told
Her friends her love. And by their true advice

She wrote her love upon a lotus leaf
With her fair rose-red nails, awhile her cheek
With pleasure thrilled and one eyebrow divine
Was raised by strength of her love's yearning thought.
She wrote her heart's sweet secret in her words.
Then stept the king within that radiant bower
And bore the answer ere the missive came.
Her friends then got from him his royal word
That she his queen would be and left them there
Bridegroom and bride by brief Gandharva rites
To taste the raptures of their youthful love.
The king then left the bower with heavy heart
And swore that he would send to her full soon
His ministers to bring her like a queen
In state. She stayed in her sweet hermitage,
Her mind with eager quickness at the feet
Of her belovéd lord in gladness laid.
The sage Durvásas came but she was lost
In thoughts of pining love and saw him not.
He cursed her that her lord would her forget.
Priyamvada then hastened unto him
And soothed his ire. He half withdrew his curse
And said that if a keepsake ornament
Were shown, the king's remembrance would be clear.

She then rejoiced as King Dushyanta's ring
Which he put on the finger of his love
Remained with her.
When Kanwa great returned
He heard with joy that sweet Sakuntala
Had wedded noble Dushyanta. Though grieved
To part with her, his heart's delight, he felt
That she as wife and mother soon to be
Must with her lord live glad in love's delights.
The Ashram matrons pure and chaste her blessed
With life's true joys in her imperial home.
The Sylvan gods, who had with tender care
Watched o'er her life, gave white and shining silks
Fair like the moon at full and lustrous gems
For her to wear. Then Kanwa came to her
With heart too full for words as he his child,
Albeit no child of his, sent far away.
Such sorrow blinds with tears the eyes of those
Who must their children send to newer homes
At duty's call. He told the trees her friends
That she who would not quench her thirst till they
Were satisfied, who would not take a leaf
Or flower from them because of her deep love,
Though fond she was of lovely things, who felt
A thrill of joy when blossoms shone in spring,
Now sought their leave to go to meet her lord.

The trees through liquid notes of *kokil* sweet
Their assent gave and wished her lasting joy.
But lingered yet the fair Sakuntala
Unwilling her dear friends to leave behind.
Her loving fawn then nestled in her dress
And would not let her go. With heavy heart
She took her dear friends' leave. And then they gave
To her Dushyanta's ring. The holy sage
Then said to her: " Revere thy elders well;
With reverence and with kindness treat thou all;
Adore thy husband as thy God; and live
A holylife of duty and of love."
She went around the sacrificial fire
And placed her golden head at Kanwa's feet
And rose to go. Two sages with her went
And with them went a lady anchorite
To take her to the king. With loving eyes
That lingered on the trees and fawns and streams
She went; a kokil sang its plaintive note;
The trees then bent their heads in sad farewell;
The fawns with large and lustrous eyes then gazed
At her retreating form.
Thus went the wife
To meet her lord. But he with clouded mind
Remembered her no more. Sakuntala

Let slip her ring while on her way she stopped
At Shacheetirtha pure for prayer. And when
They reached the palace gates, the king's command
Was brought to take them to the audience hall.
The king was grieved at their oft-urgéd claim
As he could not remember that he loved
And wedded her, and it did ill become
A pure and noble man, a king besides,
To welcome home as wife a lady fair
Who seemed a wife already by her looks
And whom he could not call to mind as his
True wedded wife. The keepsake ring was lost.
Then she her veil let fall that he her face
Might see and then remember all his love,
But his full-clouded memory could not
Find light at sight of that full-orbéd moon.
She spoke to him what tender words he said
In forest bower, but recollection clear
Came not to him. And in that royal hall
She stood with joyless heart and downcast looks.
For fate is adamant and human lives
Are but its playthings. Then rejected thus
By him and by her friends who could not take
Her back thus branded with such infamy
To their pure forest-home of praying saints,

She by her mother, nymph of happy heaven,
Was taken there from earth in airy flight.
But vague unrest and deep melancholy
Became the king's companions from that day
When he in audience hall her love denied.
Albeit the surface of his consciousness
Knew not as yet her purity and love,
Dim stirrings as of antenatal Love
Awoke in him. The keepsake ring that fell
In waters was found by a fisherman
And was by loyal servants sent to him.
The ring shone like the sun and chased away
The ling'ring clouds of darkness from his mind.
A stinging sense of shame and gnawing grief
His royal pride laid low. He chid the ring
That like him knew her fingers' nectar-touch
Yet lost that heaven. He drew her heavenly form
On canvas as when she in Ashram stood
In beauty while the ardent circling bee
Her lips and eyes and hair adored with joy,
And then as she reclined on lotus leaves
In yearning love of him. And thus in sight
Of her sweet pictured form his lifeless life
He spent who spurned her living form of heaven.
His grief had widened his love's vast domain
And made him gentler and more merciful

In his imperial rule and he proclaimed
That whoe'er lost his kin shall find in him
The love that death deprived.
Thus passed some years.
One morn a nymph, fair Sânumathi, came
To earth and saw the king's most hapless plight.
His plaintive tones of grief fell on her ears
And turned to tenderness her angry heart
That felt his treatment of Sakuntala
As cruel stab to her. In sudden flight
She went to heaven and bore the happy news.
It chanced that at this time great Indra sent
His charioteer to bring the king to heaven
To lend his aid against the Rakshasas.
The King whose love of Dharma was as deep
As his love for his fair Sakuntala
Laid by his grief and took his mighty bow
And went in Indra's chariot unto heaven.
The golden car flew like a rising star
Till all the vast and varied earth did seem
A speck of dust. He on the fields of heaven
The powers of darkness vanquished with his arms
And shone above the crimson waves of war.
But yet he bore in heart a gnawing grief
As she the light of eyes and joy of heart
Had been put by with cruel mocking words,

And he could see no more her lotus face
And hear her silver tones of tender love
And live in her love's perfect paradise.
The heav'n where he victorious stood in arms
No heav'n to him did seem who lost love's heaven.
The radiant light that shone in splendour there
From golden sun and never-waning moon
To him seemed gloom who her love's radiance [lost.
The never-fading flowers that blossomed there
Seemed nought to him who lost her flower-soft feet.
The wondrous music of the nymphs of heaven
Jarred on the ears that could not gladly hear
Her voice far sweeter than the *Kokil's* note.
A sudden throb of shoulder brought him joy
Though there was not a cause therefor. He saw
A boy of perfect beauty there in play
Who dragged a lion's whelp with sportive power
From its dread mother, Ah! this wondrous boy
Who was incarnate grace and strength combined,
On whose imperial forehead sat the power
That rules the world by might of righteous will,
What happy parent did this treasure own?
This childless king felt for the noble boy
A love that drew him with resistless power.

The boy felt sweet responsive love in him.
A wreath worn by the boy had fallen down.
The king to take it bent. The lady pure
Who came there with the boy, in trembling tones
Forbade to take the charméd amulet
As it if touched by one save those who gave
The boy his birth would turn a serpent fierce
And strike. But ere she spake, the king the wreath
Had taken in his hands and it shone there
A fragrant wreath. He asked her then: "This boy
My heart attracts with potent love. What line
Is happy by his birth?". She said: "He is
Of Puru's noble race". He then embraced
The boy and felt as if all heaven lay
In that sweet touch of frame to loving frame.
The lady wondered at their likeness true.
The king desired to ask who bore the boy
As God's sweet gift but could not make his tongue
The request utter, as another's wife
Can ne'er be thought of by one pure of soul.
A lady brought a bright toy peacock there
And said by chance to that sweet-featured boy:
"Ah see this bright Sakunta's (bird's) loveliness."
The boy whose mother was a thought divine
That always shone in his adoring heart

Her asked : " Where is my mother dear?." The word
Had taken unto her his loving mind.
A sudden gladness of assurance came
To great Dushyanta's agonised mind.
He held the bright-eyed boy in close embrace
And shed sweet tears of joy. Then came his [Queen,
The queen of his fair realm, his heart, his soul.
Fair Sanumathi's words had brought sweet hope
To her who lived a dead and cheerless life.
She came with settled gloom upon her face
And faded cheeks where once the living gold
Of life's bright tint brought heav'n to human eyes.
The light divine of beauty bright shone there
Though its fair roseate morning hues had gone.
A soiled garment clad her perfect limbs.
With downcast looks and winning modest grace
She came to see her child and found both child
And lord. The King her pardon sweet besought,
But she no words of self-reproach would hear.
She said : " Blame not thy noble self, my Lord.
My sins in other births had parted me
From thy true love's eternal paradise.
The Gods have turned their ire to tender grace
And smile upon my truth. A wondrous bliss

Far sweeter than our pure love's early joy
Has come to me, unworthy that I am.
My lord, I weep to see that thy bright face
Has lost through grief its royal glance and mien.
Ah wretched me that could not go ere now
To wipe thy tears and make thy noble heart
A realm of bliss divine !". The King replied :
" Ah perfect love that knows no thought of self
But in a rapture of renouncing gives
Its sweetness ripe with glad abounding joy,
How god-like is thy grace of golden heart
As thy fair form is full of light divine!
What cruel words I flung at thee, my love,
At thee the marvel of the world of truth !
But they have by the magic of thy love
Come back to me as blessings true and sweet.
Ah let this noble boy who brought to me
The promise of thy true forgiving love
Plead with thy heart and win it back to me."
His words brought soothing joy, and blinding tears
Of gladness blotted out the world of woe
That spread grief's darkness all around before.
He touched her cheek with soft caressing hands
And her frame thrilled with joy and then re-born
In love she stood a blooming goddess there,
As when bright *Shri* was born in days of yore

And blessed the world with beauty and with love.
He placed his ring upon her finger fair again
As symbol of re-union sweet. And then they went
To sage Marichi and his blessings got.
And then they with their darling child returned
To earth and lived in splendour and in joy
In this bright land whose sweet auspicious name
The world took from the blessed name of him
Who was the son of sweet Sakuntala
And her true loving heart's self-chosen King.

SAMYUKTA.

I sing a lay of those forgotten days
While yet a knightlier godlier life in peace
And war did linger fondly on our land—
Where Rama pure and Krishna sweet did come,
Incarnate God-head from deep love of man,
To lead him to the Heaven of Love and Peace
Through gradual gracious steps of service glad,
Of pure devotion, and of wisdom true:
Where manly men and pure-souled women fair
Within the Dharma's gracious heavenly round
Rejoicing lived and died: where love and joy
Drew with their subtle yet resistless ties
The social groups of Ind. that knew the art—
Not elsewhere known and now forgotten here—
Of moving forward with unfaltering feet
With one heart beating in their diverse frames:
Where grim Aggression's dire unsated greed
Spread ne'er its baleful shade on earth: where strong
To keep the gracious gifts of smiling heaven
The Aryans lived with God-word passion dowered
And perfect self-control that robed in fair

Art's silken vestments woven bright by peace
Their mighty limbs rejoicing in their power:
Where rose bright shines as if to reach the skies
And bring sweet gospels true from far-off heaven
To waiting men below: where Ganga pure
With waving mantle white and vocal feet
And singing mouth that taught Truth's mystic lore
Sped through the land, and in her four bright hands
Bore gifts of truth and peace and love and joy:
O'er whose fair plains the king of mountains shone
And kept his gracious watch, his summits white
Receiving e'er the sun's first golden touch:
Around whose frame the blue and shining seas
Flung their protecting arms with eager love:
Which full-dowered thus with outer splendours bright
And inner raptures shone like paradise.

Of sweet Samyukta and her knightly lord
I sing: their love that conquered death and shone,
A star with stainless radiance lit for ever
Above the restless crimson waves of war:
Their sweet and shining lives that always turned
Upon the poles of duty and of love
And moved in one bright orbit lit and warmed
By central sun of godliness supreme:

Their deep devotion to their land of birth
That knew no sacrifice for her too great
And gladly proudly felt in cheerless death
For her the sweet fulfilment of the dreams
That dominated all their lives.
There lived
In mighty Kanouj in those ancient times
A Princess fair beyond a poet's dreams
When by a silver stream in evening hour
He sits and sees the sunset palaces
Far-shining with a wondrous wealth of tints
In western skies and sees a vision dawn
Upon his mind of her, the reigning queen
That shines in state in those sweet sunset realms
And whose sweet fascination on him grows
When night doth dower the world with speechless charm.

He sees the crescent of her forehead bright,
Her star-like eyes and sweet celestial grace,
And feels his pulses quicken, heart beat fast,
And knows that thenceforth she to him will be
The soul of his adoring soul. Thus shone
Samyukta sweet upon the world, and dowered
All hearts with love that knew no taint of self
But full of reverent thankfulness did praise
The Lord for lighting human eyes and hearts

With beauty such as hers: so pure, so fair
She was. Though she was rarely seen by all
The fame of her bright beauty spread after
Like perfume of the golden *Champak* flowers
When spring returns and yearning earth is glad.
Far sweeter than the smiling nymphs of heaven
And pure in heart like Sita, Savitri,
Usha, Sakuntala, or Droupathi,
She was the lotus 'mid fair woman-flowers.
She had a noble matchless strength of soul
That was her dower by birth in Rajput line.
For not unused to red war's fierce alarms
She used to hear with glad quick-beating heart
And shining eyes of deeds of valour done
By her brave kinsmen, and the warrior knights
Took keen delight while yet she was a girl
In seeking her approval and applause
And thrilled her willing ears with stories true
Of knightly valour and chivalrous deeds.
Thus strong in soul and true of heart, with mind
Full blossomed 'neath the genial warmth of rays
Of learning and of arts, and fair in frame
That had both strength and grace, Samyukta stood
At that sweet junction where the blended charms
Of girlhood sweet and sweeter womanhood
Did meet and dowered her with a form of heaven.

And Prithvi Raj, fair Delhi's sovereign lord,
Far famed for his heroic knightly deeds
Again and yet again of her he heard.
Her praise sung by the tuneful bards did bear
His heart on shining wings of song and rhyme
To her. A helpless captive of her charms
He stood before the lady of his dreams.
He dimly felt that love had come to him
With its commingled gift of bliss and pain.
He then his foster-mother sought and told
Her of his passion for the unseen fair:
"Ah mother, would'st thou save me from my pain
And make me glad?" She fondly answered: "Yes.
What ails thee now, my child?" He slowly said
With hesitation born of youthful love
Absorbed in golden dreams of joy and shy
Of speaking out its soul lest loveless ears
Be deaf to its sweet melody, while pain
That sprang from hopeless love did urge him on
To seek swift help and comfort: "Often have
I heard from sweet-mouthed bards in songs and rhymes
Samyukta's peerless regal loveliness.
And often in my happiest dreams her form
Imagined by my wakeful soul has shone

A full-orbed moon on sleep's sweet summer night
And even in my waking hours I feel
The world around me full of hints of her.
The southern breezes seem to whisper sweet
About the fragrance of her flower-crowned hair.
The crimson morning glows that speed along
As swift as thought from chambers of the east
And glad proclaim to all the waiting worlds
The Sun-God coming in his golden car
Illume my mind with vision of her smiles.
The sweet full moon that gently comes in light
Attended by the stars to reign in state
In skies that yearn to feel her silver feet
With blissful tread brings dreams of her fair face."
With anxious love ashining in her eyes
She heard the king's confession of his love
And said to him: "The gracious gods will smile
Upon thy passion, son. As thou, for might,
So she, for beauty sweet, is praised of all.
I saw her once in her sweet girlish days.
She was a vision of ethereal grace,
A summer-dream of some sweet-hearted bard
Who sees the goddess of his soul before him shine
Upon his love's pure throne and goes through life
With praying lips and bright adoring eyes
That see the full moon of her shining face

Shine bright in Fancy's topmost central blue
And see not nor e'er care to see the shows
Of life. When some one told her whence I came
And that I was the nurse of Delhi's Prince—
Thou wert a god-like boy in those sweet days,
The light of my fond eyes, my heart's delight—
She bent her noble head before my feet.
I asked her half in jest if she would wed
My darling prince. She looked within my eyes
With smiling glowing eyes, and then she glanced
At her dear mother, Queen of Kanouj great.
Her mother smiled approval, and I said:
"Samyukta dear! I know not whom the Lord
Has chosen as the sovereign of thy charms.
But sure to be thy chosen husband dear
Is better than the Kingship of the earth.
My boy is Prithviraj, the King of earth,
And nothing has he on this earth to win
But thee far sweeter than all Empires are."
And with a far-off wistful tender gaze
And happy mist of tears in her sweet eyes
She sighed and silent kept. Ah thus I was
Unconscious prophet of the coming joys.
I shall do all within my power, my son,
To bring to full fruition thy great love."

And on a calm and fragrant summer morn

She in a litter left for Delhi town.
Through many towns renowned in martial song
She passed to Kanouj, Queen of cities fair,
Beyond Kalindi stream, dark-blue by birth
And made more ravishingly dark and fair
By contact with the sweet and shining frame
Of Krishna. Then she reached that radiant town
At nightfall when the calm and regnant moon
Sent down to earth a flood of silver light
And turned all hearts to love's delicious joys.
The foster-mother Ganga knew full well
That entrance she could never gain at all
If she admission sought as one who came
From Delhi. Jaichand, King of Kanouj great,
Then on a universal conquest bent
Had carried his victorious arms to realms
Both far and near, till Màndalika crowned
He owned the homage of the Aryan world.
But Prithviraj resisted Jaichand's arms
And owned no mortal suzerain. Inflamed
By this resistance to his sovereign power
Jaichand had decreed death to all who came
From Delhi to his famous Kanouj town.
Samyukta was to Ganga like the gem
That shines upon a hooded serpent's head.
So Ganga entered service as a servant-maid

In Jaichand's palace great and served with love
The Princess fair. So sweet her heart and ways
That fair Samyukta came to look on her
With almost filial love. And Ganga loved
Her mistress young with deep and jealous love
Which sweet Samyukta lit in all true hearts.
She would prepare the scented bath and dress
Samyukta's heavenly frame in shining silks
That softer were than roseleaf to the touch,
And put the *thilak* on her moon-like face
And paint her feet with bright vermilion paint.
She ne'er could at her lady gaze enough,
So great her love, so bright her lady's face.
She oft would read the storied wonders past—
Of Sita, Savitri, and Droupadi,
Of true Sukanya, sweet Sakuntala,
Of Damayanthi and the Yaksha's wife—
And saw the heaven of sweet Samyukta's heart
Reflected in her face when those bright tales
She heard. And often in the gardens fair
Where slow-paced breezes brought the bliss of heaven
With gentle perfume and with coolness dowered
When spring laughed bright from trees in radiant bloom
Together they would stroll. To holy shrines

They both would go with eager hearts and feet
To worship Vani, Shri, or Gouri fair.
So some months passed. Samyukta could not bear
A moment's separation from her maid
And Ganga told her many wonderous tales
Of Ancient India which the blessed feet
Of God himself made pure and then she spoke
With joy and pride about the Delhi line.
And during moon-lit nights upon the top
Of her fair palace sweet Samyukta lay
And drank with thirsting ears the tales she heard.
And like the gracious whisper of the morn
To dreaming virgin earth of love and light
From bridegroom sun in golden raiment clad—
He comes with gracious royal look and sees
Adoring worlds salute His godlike might
And smiles on them but looks with boundless love
Upon the fruitful sweetness of the earth—
Was Ganga's talk to sweet Samyukta's ears.
When Ganga spoke of Prithiviraj she feared
That Jaichand's hate his daughter too might share,
But sweet Samyukta said: "Oh mother mine,
Once in my girlhood did I hear of him
From his own nurse who spoke of her bright boy

With god-like forehead bright and gracious speech.
I know not how it is that though I never
Have looked on him, I seem to know him well!"
This Ganga heard with joy, for those two lives
That she loved most—like those twin streams that rise
From God's beloved home, Himalaya,
The white-clad Ganga and the Jumna blue,
Which flow with dim foreknowledge of the joys
Of coming union and their waters sweet
Commingling flow in one refulgent stream
With gifts of godly life and wealth's increase
To Aryavarta's proud and smiling plains—
Did feel the sweet compulsion of desire
And had previsions dim of coming joys
And faint sweet sense of antenatal love.
And Ganga then before Samyukta's eyes
A portrait placed of Delhi's sovereign king.
With shyness and with love Samyukta's face
A picture of confusion sweet became.
She would not take the portrait nor would yet
Let Ganga take it back. Then Ganga left
Her on some pretext and the portrait lay
Neglected on the terrace bright. But soon
Samyukta with her soul in her sweet eyes
Pored on the pictured face of Prithivi Raj

And felt sweet kinship with him though unseen.
Alone beneath the glory of the moon
She lay with silence compass'd round, forgot
Her father's spacious realms and kingly power,
Her rank and beauty sweet, and only felt
In some dim past she loved fair Delhi's king
Though how or when or where she did not know.
And some days later Ganga yearned to go
To Delhi. Then she told her Princess dear
What brought her into Kanouj and from where
And who she was. She said: " O Princess mine,
I am that nurse of Delhi's sovereign Prince
Of whom you spoke. From stories of thy grace,
Thy large bright eyes and face like golden moon,
The sweetness of thy soul, he yearns to win
Thy heart's sweet paradise. Ah how could he
Communicate to thee his heart's desire?
I strove to help him and to know thy will.
How does your heart incline? For your reply
Will kill or crown him. Ah! Wilt thou forgive
My hiding of my name and wish from thee?"
The Princess turned on her those star-like eyes
That kindled deep desire with dreaming gaze
And said: " I know not, mother, what to say.
Thou knowest well I love thy noble Prince
Albeit he ne'er has shone upon my eyes.

I feel an ancient passion come to life
In some mysterious way whene'er my eyes
Dwell on his pictured eyes and face and form.
I feel most shy and full of shame to tell
Thee this but thou dost love me well and I
Do love thee as I loved my mother dear.
But know thou well and let my heart's king know
That my dear father's hate of him is deep
As is my love! Ah let my Lord forget
That I exist and hold his course on earth
As sun in skies to dower the world with light
And warmth and happiness. I shall not wed
At all, and if my father urges me
To wed, I shall the gracious aid of Death
Most gladly seek to go in haste to heaven
And wait for my dear lord till he doth rise
To those serenest heights of Paradise."
While thus in mournful and melodious tones
She gave her message, Ganga's heart was full
Of mingled grief and joy. Love's gracious tears
Stood in her eyes when she admiring saw
Conflicting love and duty in the face
Of sweet Samyukta. Then she took her leave
To go, and promised soon again to come.

By this time Jaichand had with soaring pride
Resolved to celebrate the *Soenair* rite.

The rules of this great sacrifice required
That every place and function none can hold
From cooks and porters to the highest men—
But kings. Since those heroic spacious times
When Dharmaraja and his sinless kin
Did justly rule a subjugated world
And glad performed full well this regal rite
With leave of Krishna—Godhead incarnate—
No prince had soared so high in e'en his dreams
As thought of e'er performing such a rite.
Not even Vikrama who ruled the earth
By force of arms and with benignant sway,
With whom an era new and great began,
At whose Court shone the nine bright gems of thought—
To such a glorious sacrifice aspired.
But Jaichand overshadowed by his fate
And India's destiny resolved—alas—
Upon performance of the sacrifice.
He had resolved to close the regal rite
With his Samyukta's sweet *Swayamvara*.
And so messengers from his Court were sent
To distant realms to bear his mandates great.
But Jaichand would not invite Prithvi Raj
As they were mortal foes and Delhi's king
His power supreme defied with god-like might.

The Princess knew the wedding to be near
And felt like one condemned to death. Her heart
Was hers no more to give or hold at will.
She her dear lord had chosen in her heart
And flung the garland of her fancy-flowers
Around the neck of her most gracious king.
She had no hope of happy wifehood sweet
And gracious heavenly laughter of a child.
She prayed to Shri to let the bitter cup
Untasted pass and grant auspicious days.
Thus in despairing mood she grieving lived.
But Prithviraj when he the happy news
Of Sweet Samyukta's coming marriage heard
Felt lifted to the throne of peerless joy,
Crowned with her sweet-toned words of heavenly love
And sceptred with her pure and loving thoughts.
He felt no more despondent or unstrung.
For mighty and girt round by heroes great
He felt no doubt of conquering Jaichand's arms
And bear her willing captive of his might.

The sacrificial day came near. And then
The king decreed that his great rival's effigy
Should stand as porter in the sacred hall
As mark of deep dishonour and his hate,
And this was done. Samyukta knew not this.
The sacrifice was over. And the wedding day
Drew near. In that great town where men from far

Had come in millions, no one knew or guessed
That Prithviraj and his most mighty knights
Strong clad in mail in silken garments hid
Had mingled in the crowd and watched their time.
It came. In that great city, gorgeous, fair
With its ten thousand thousand houses bright,
Large crowds of men in holiday attire
Kept seemly mirth. A blaze of colour bright
Made paradise of that most lovely town.
From windows in the houses shining bright
Fair maidens dowered with beauty, decked with gems
And dressed in silks, forgot Zenana rules
And shone upon the world beneath their feet.
And Prithviraj impelled by sweet revenge
For Jaichand's slighting him in public gaze
And by his passion for the princess fair,
Had brought the flower of his renownéd knights
To take his bride by force and cover with shame
Great Jaichand's most presumptuous sacrifice.

At length did dawn the day of nuptial choice,
And universal jubilation shone
In that bright town. Th' assembled princes all
In gorgeous raiments clad, with flashing gems
Upon their crowns and jewels took their seats
In that most fair and spacious audience hall
Which art and nàture decked like paradise.
The Princess fair was soon to come and choose

The sovereign of her heart. Upon a dais
Beneath a canopy of crimson silk
Apparent king of kings great Jaichand shone.
And at the farthest end of that vast hall
The hideous effigy of Prithviraj
In wooden homage most neglected stood
As porter of the hall, while far beyond
Vast surging crowds of eager townsmen moved
Like seas in storms. With them commingled stood
With flashing eyes and armed in triple mail
Beneath their peaceful outward vestments fair,
The King of Delhi and his martial kinghts
To win the Princess fair as Vikrama
Won Urvasi from Asuras of yore.
His bard, great Chand, with him disguiséd stood.

A sudden hush prevailed, for through a door
Were heard the music sweet of anklets bright
And gentle rustling of refulgent silks.
And soon as comes with silver steps and grace
The moon in beauty to th' expectant skies
With her far-shining groups of vestal stars,
Samyukta came with all her maids around.
A dress of crimson silk around her form
In loving undulations fondling twined—
Fit emblem of the flame of passion bright
Which she enkindled in all knightly hearts.
And priceless diamonds, sapphires, rubies, pearls,

Adorned her form. Her face was like the moon
When in full-orbéd glory in the skies
Apparent queen she moves in soverign state.
But on this great auspicious day a veil
Did like an envious cloud obscure its light.
But it could never hide the matchless grace,
The sweet symmetry of her shining form,
The beauty of her timid swanlike gait
And feet that shone like golden lotuses
With anklets that unceasing sang of them
And their sweet arch of instep and of grace.
The bangles round her wrists her arms did praise
And made harmonious answer. Thus she came
Before th' assembled knighthood of the land
In that far-shining hall of nuptial choice.
But in her heart did dwell deep-seated woe.
She knew that her belovéd king and lord
Was hated of her father and disgraced
In that presumptuous sacrifice. But yet
She did not know where her King's image stood.
That morning she had prayed in Shri's bright shrine
To guide her through the perils of the day.
A royal maiden making nuptial choice
Could choose her lord from kings assembled there.
But showing unto all that her dear lord
Was some one absent from the nuptial hall—
How could a maid and that a Princess great

Do this? With throbbing head and beating heart
And feet that most unwilling moved, she came
With marriage garland of bright fragrant flowers
In flowersoft hands. But once within that hall
The warrior blood in her gave strength and power
To face the ordeal that her cruel fate
Ordained for her. The blare of trumpets ceased.
Her heralds went before their Princess fair
And asked the hearlds of each royal knight
Who had most gladly come to win the hand
And heart of sweet Samyukta who he was.
Before the shining thrones of many kings
Her radiant form a moment stood and lit
With beauty bright the dark surrounding space.
But with soft steps and sinuous movements fair
She passed the thrones that in a deeper gloom
Were wrapt when her form's golden lamp from them
Did go away. At last the Princess came
To where the image of her Prithviraj
Neglected stood with mocking crown of thorns.
She put aside her fear and bashfulness
In one great mood of daring loving supreme,
And decked the image with her garland bright
In token of her choice. The men assembled there
In breathless consternation viewed the scene.
Then burst the angry and imperial tones
Of Jaichand's on the silence. "What! hast thou,

The perfect blossom of my noble line
Thus stooped to fall upon the charnel house
Of my most hated rival's petty throne!"
But ere his words could fall from quivering lips
King Prithviraj upon his charger placed
The shrinking princess fair and girt with knights
Flashed like a meteor through the seeking crowd.
Through Jaichand's soldiers them pursued, the prize
Of perfect love was borne by Prithviraj.
And decked with roses of victorious war
And lotus flowers of his victorious love
He came in glory back to his domain.
Samyukta's wedded life was one long day
Of smiling joy lit by the golden sun
Of sovereign power and by the silver moon
Of perfect love.
        But soon the day of doom
Came from the waiting store of future days.
Mahomed Ghori came with conquering arms
And offered war. And matchless Prithviraj
To meet the foe in battle yearned. His queen
Though she him captive held in silken chains
Of yearning love felt her rich Rajput blood
Enkindling in her frame and on her lord
She buckled knightly armour with her hands
And with her sainted smile to victory
Her king she sent. He came with honour back

To her fair golden arms. In love's sweet joy
Time flew with dancing quickness. But again
Mahomed Ghori came with bigger hosts.
And with his arms great Jaichand's arms were joined
And sweet Samyukta's prayers nought availed.
Upon the battlefield while yet the hosts
Had not been hurled in mortal shock of arms,
Samyukta hastened to her father's tent
In garments knightly dressed. She met him there
And said: "Can you not turn thy heart away
From this most fatal act that at one stroke
Thy daughter and thy land deprives of life?
If not, my prayers fight with my sweet lord
Against my country's and my Dharma's foes.
I crave thy blessing." He then turned his face
Away and with his guilty conscience bent
His head in speechless shame. But he had sworn
To slake his thirst of vengeance in the stream
Of war, and blinding passion soiled his soul.
Samyukta hastened to her waiting lord
And said that hope was none except in heaven.
He shed some manly tears in thought of her
Whose purity and love so well deserved
An endless round of sweet unclouded joys,
And her most hapless fate and of his land
That was the holiest land in all the earth
And its unhappy undeservéd doom.

Samyukta wiped his tears and cheered his heart
With comfort that her inner heart had not.
She buckled on his armour and sent forth
Her lord and his great armies to the field of war.
She and her maids and all the people there
Kept fast and vigil praying unto God
To bless with conquest's joys his mighty arms.
Alas for human hopes and human prayers!
The hour of fate had struck. And Delhi's king
And India's sovereign power lay low in dust.
Samyukta heard the fatal news. The fire
She kindled there and through its portals bright
She went to meet her noble lord in heaven.

VISHNUPRIYA.

In Gour far-famed for smile of golden corn
Where Ganga pure with fair white robes doth speed
With gifts of outer wealth and inner Joy,
And where Himalaya lifts high our thoughts
To God's sweet lotus feet, there lived a maid,
Vishnupriya by name. She was a flower
That shone amidst the many weeds of life.
She grew in beauty by the holy stream
Like some sweet jasmine flower by sun and dew
Most gladly nursed yet rooted in the earth.
And when she reached the age of maidenhood,
Ere yet love whispered body's thrilling bliss
In her pure heart, her parents chose her God
To whom her body, mind, and heart and soul
Were precious adoration flowers divine.
To him whom afterwards the worlds adored
As Chaitanya she was the wedded wife.
In gladness moved the joyful wedded years.
Nimai, for learning and for beauty famed
—Such was his name before the orange robe
He wore—became the idol of his town—
Fair Nawadwip where Learning's Goddess shone
And lit the light of law and love in all,—
And learners from the ends of India came

To bathe their bodies in the Ganga sweet
And minds and hearts in that far holier stream
Of Godward thought and love that ceaseless flows
From Scripture's high and white Himalayas
That touch with topmost peaks God's lotus feet.
He taught the learners that from far and near
From him sought knowledge of the truth of things
From holy scriptures and from wise men's words.
Thus moved the mingled lives of these pure souls,
Fair Vishnupriya and her blessèd lord.
But soon a new light shone before his eyes;
A sweeter rapture dawned within his heart.
God's love bright like the silver moon at full
Arose in his mind's vast o'er-arching sky
Lit with a million stars of learning's gifts,
And shone with steadfast splendour queen o'er all.
The love of God o'erbore all earthly love
As when the pure resistless flood doth come
From melted snows, the petty struggling stream
Meandering through the Ganga's golden bed
In shallow sparkling grace is hurried on
To meet and mingle with the ocean vast.
One day he went to Ganga where he saw
Sri Krishna's holy footprints on a rock.
A sudden rapture filled his soul. A stream
Of happy tears fed at the fountain sweet
Of his pure soul flowed from his shining eyes.

The crowd around him like the swelling sea
Beneath the full moon's calm and loving gaze,
Or like the surging thoughts of love and joy
That are enkindled in a lover's heart
When his belovéd looks with loving eyes,
Felt blissfull thrills of God-love's raptures sweet,
When they around him stood, they lost in love
Divine of Him and he in love of God.

That day was born in him the bliss of love
That shone a lighted splendour in his heart
Through life. He was the same yet not the same
As heretofore. The love of God that shone
In him all lesser loves bore down. His wife
Unknowing yet the bliss of love of God
That gives true fullness unto life and love
Looked on the strange and speechless ecstacy
That lit his eyes and face and golden frame
But him oblivious made of all the stress
And storm and petty cares and joys of life.
With anxious love's devoted deep concern
She saw with mute and eager love his ways
And words and his ecstatic trances sweet.
She knew that he was wise and that his love
For her was true and deep and knew no bounds.
She knew not what to do but hastening went
To Lakshmi's shrine. She prayed for help divine
To lead her husband's heart to her again.

"O Goddess bright, that knowést human hearts
Ere they their true desires in words declare!
I pray thou turn his heart again to me.
I know not what has turned it far from home
And all the sweet familiar tasks and joys
And holy sanctities of earlier life.
Thou art my only refuge and my hope".
With new composure and expectant heart
She turned her golden footsteps home. She found
Her well-belovéd lord with lotus eyes
Half-closed in contemplation deep of God.
Then with adoring eyes she waited there
For his sweet smiling looks and sweet-toned words.
He opened his half-closed God-seeing eyes
And saw his wife. A sudden tenderness
His soul with deeper love for her inspired.
He asked her: "What has made thy lotus face
Its wonted freshness and its beauty lack?
Ah, tell me, sweet, if aught upon thy mind
Doth heavy sit. Upon thy face should shine
Its wonted brightness wreathed in radiant smiles."
She said: "My lord, why dost thou thus thy days
And nights in prayers and in vigils spend
That mar the beauty of thy golden frame?"
And he replied: "O dearest one, a love
Far sweeter than the love whose light
Thy golden hands lit in this graceless heart

Now sways my thoughts and in my soul doth shine.
My thoughts have turned to Him whose heavenly have
Is sweeter than all earthly life and love.
Lord Krishna in my heart His light divine
Has lit. I love not less my perfect wife
But love Sir Krishna more." She then in words
That showed her love and duty struggling hard
For power in her most pure yet passionate heart:
"What knows thy slave about the Godward way?
I know but one sweet God and that art thou.
What you ordain is gospel truth to me.
I know and seek no higher holier truth.
Go thou thy Godward way and let me come
Behind thee with my glad adoring eyes
As Sita followed Rama great before."
From day to day he grew in love of God
And love of man. And soon his holy fame
From land to land did spread as Spring's sweet charm
With quick tread goes from East to waiting West.
He was incarnate love and with pure gaze
And loving speech and soft compassionate heart
He lifted all the world to love of God.
One day he sought his blesséd mother's leave
To take *Sanyása* and in search of God
To go to sacred sweet Brindavana.
His mother Shachee torn 'twixt love for him
And for his happiness tried hard to keep

His eager thoughts at home in bondage sweet
By asking how he could desert his wife,
Who had then gone to her paternal house.
The news that her belovéd lord his home
Might leave in glad and yearning love of God
To Vishnupriya went. With faltering feet
And drooping heart she came. The sun had set,
And to the bridal room where slept her lord
She went and saw him wrapt in slumber deep.
She placed his lotus feet upon her lap
And gazed upon his golden lotus face
In sweet and speechless love. A flood of tears
From her with joy and grief commingled came.
A few drops fell upon his feet. His eyes
Then opened and a sudden tender light
Of joy flashed from those shining orbs of love.
He asked: "My love, why do the clouds of grief
Thus hide thy heart's pure sky lit by the moon
Of love and by the stars of pure bright thoughts?"
He then divined what fears had shadows thrown
Upon her sunlit path, and sought by words
To his heart's truest friend his plan of life
Declare. A sudden glory dazzling shone
About his form, and she a power divine—
Great Vishunu's self—saw there in light revealed.
She bowed in deep devotion and to God
Prayed that He would her husband's love incline

To her again. Then Vishnu's form divine
Disappeared and her lord she saw again.
He wondered at her love that gladly chose
His love as higher than attaining God.
He then to soothe her heart with gentle words
Began: "My loving wife! Such love as thine
Is sweet beyond expression unto me.
Wouldst thou not help to save the sinful world
In suffering steeped, and even with thy tears
Wash out the sins and crimes and griefs of men.
If for God's work we tread our diverse ways,
Our lives are still but one as e'er before.
I shall for ever live within thy heart
Though I thy sweet side leave to save the world?"
A higher holier mood to her then came
And she her glad consent rejoicing gave
To let him go, to save the suffering world.
Such is love's power to kindle Love Divine.

A few days passed in utter deep delight.
Then came the night that was the last of all
When earthly love's small silver lamp of light
Its gentle radiance shed about their feet.
In bright silks clad most gay and fair to see,
With lustrous gems that with their beauty shone
On her more lustrous frame, she moved about
The house with holy rapture in her heart.
That night when she upon his bosom slept

He kissed her tenderly and then arose
And left the house and went with eager feet
To the wide world beyond. She felt a chill
And shivering rose and found that he had gone.
She called his mother dear in tones of grief.
Then Shachee came and saw the weeping wife
Stand dazed against the wall. Then Nitai come—
The Lord's true friend—and went in search of him.
Meantime Shachee and Vishnupriya sat
Determined not to taste or food or drink
Till news came from their best beloved one.
Soon Nitai came and told how his loved friend
Had taken ásram and at Santipur
To meet his early friends and townsmen stayed.
His mother was to come but not his wife.
With heavy heart whose deep and speechless grief
Her anklets spoke she turned and went within,
While all around her suffered for her grief.
But even ere they had sweet sight of him
His lustrous form and loving lotus eyes
Shone in her heart. Thus days succeeded days.
Shachee returned but came without her son.
Five years thus passed and then there came the news
That Chaitanya—such was the Lord's new name—
Was coming to Navadvip his former home.
A thousand saints and lovers true of God
His golden feet with gladness came behind.

In front of his old house he stayed awhile.
Then Shachee came and made obeisance meet
To him, but none his wife expected there.
A veilèd form before him came and fell
At his sweet lotus feet and then he said
To her: "Love Krishna" And she asked: "O lord
Some token of thy grace to this thy slave
Accord" He said: "I nothing own".
She said: "Leave me thy sandals". These he left,
And she upon her head them placed with joy
As on a throne and with slow ling'ring feet
Returned to live in worship of her lord.
That was their last sweet meeting on the earth.
He won the Lord and she won God in him.
And those pure sandals touched by his pure feet
And worshipped by pure Vishnupriya's hand
Are by glad millions worshipped to this day.

SNEHALATA.

She had but lovely frame and loving heart
As dower : for she was born of parents poor
Who lived the simple stainless life of old
And knew not newborn ways of winning wealth
By swift unholy means. One house they had,
And lived from day to day in joy and peace
On what their labour hard could find for them.
The days in bright procession came and found
Year after year their lives with gladness crowned
And grateful love to God for all His gifts
To them.
They deemed their sweet and precious child
As His most priceless gift. By that sweet name
Snehalata – the creeper of true love –
They called the child. She was a lovely girl,
A human lotus flower that shone supreme
In radiant, fresh, and stainless loveliness
Amidst surrounding mire, and lifted sweet
Her shining frame and her sweet golden soul
For Love-Sun's bright caress with eager beams.
The daily pageants of unheeded skies
That show God's grace and might ; the sudden dawn
Of beauty bright in leaf and bud and bloom
When Spring doth come in joy with heavenly feet

At whose sweet touch the dark and joyless earth
Is crowned with flowers; the bright impetous flow
Of her swift village stream when showers of rain
Bring coolness, life, and joy to thirsting earth;
And other wonders of the earth and sky,
She watched with growing love that brought new light
To her bright oval face, and rapture new
To her pure stainless soul. The village bards
Who read the lives of Ram and Krishna great—
Incarnate Godhead that with blessed feet
Did make more sacred this sweet sacred land
And reestablished Dharma on his throne
And showed Devotion true the Godward way—
Her mind ennobled with their lofty words
That winged with music soared o'er walls of sin
And selfish thought that men in blindness built
To keep God's word without lest it should shame
Their darkness with its light. She heard the tale
Of her who conquered death with heavenly love,
Who weak yet strong with strength lent by the soul
In gladness strode behind the awful Form
That armed with noose compels the souls of men
To leave their frames and bitter harvests reap
Of pleasant sins unheeding sown; of her
Who born in purple, and with bridal dress
Still shining on her young and graceful limbs
And flower-soft feet that walked on silks and flowers,

Forsaking all her pomp and splendour bright
And walking clad in barks through forests dark
With large eyes full of joy and love behind
Her Lord ; of her the forest-maiden sweet
Who Kanwa's *áshram* lit with radiance bright
And then her sisters sweet—the large-eyed deer
And flowering creepers—left at Duty's call
To meet her heart's trueking ; of her who loved
Her Lord and put aside the proferred love
Of Gods and chose the heaven of Nala's heart
Discarding deathless life in heavenly realms
With fadeless flowers. The pretty village shrine
Where Gouri, loved of brides and matrons, shines
In light—as Bála in her girlish grace,
As sweet Ambá with mother's love for all—
Did draw her golden feet day after day.
In household ways well trained, with hands
That service did not scorn but yearned to help,
And frame that lacked not strength despite its grace
And soft and rounded limbs, she shone the light
Of her sweet village home, her mother's joy,
Her father's pride.

Alas ! these wicked days !

Her brethren know not laws of God nor laws
That love for men doth frame from time to time.
They selfish , proud, preferring private good
To good of all, set laws of God at naught.

Their manhood lost, their ancient treasures lost,
They yet like stage kings shine in tinsel dress,
And speak though beggared in their head and heart
In accents large at which the world derides.
And some from these unholy ranks have come
With nostrums new for all the social ills,
And would the temples of our inner life
Destroy to build their petty chapels there.
Alas! that none should know the cure! Our youths
Their souls ill-bred on worthless inner fare
Do grow with sapless frames, and half-trained minds,
And untrained wills, and souls within them dead.
Shall we be wise in time!

This fair sweet girl
With face like the moon at full, with eyes
Large, lustrous, tender, 'neath her arched brows,
With silk-soft cheeks and rose-red lips that smiled
Above the dimpled chin—so perfect-sweet
From head crowned with her flowing tresses dark
To golden feet so fair and small—gave grief,
Not joy, to her dear parents who did seek
To crown their life by giving as their gift
Her sweetness to some worthy youth. But men
Around had beasts become that with their snouts
Did turn up earth in search of fancied wealth,
And had no eyes for treasures bright in skies
Or earth or human face or mind or heart.

She had no dowry great to make her fair
In their dim half-blind eyes that learning had
Of lustre robbed without the gift of light
To heart and sôul. She had no silks and gems
But her soft cheeks and silken tresses dark
And star-like eyes. No jewels decked her frame,
But yet in her the jewel of her soul
Outshone the Kohinoor. She had no lands
As dower but only paradise of love.
Ah who will wed her?

Long her father searched,
And far and wide he went to seek a youth
To wed his girl. For though the poet says
'A gem seeks not an owner but is sought'
This precious human gem uncared for lay.
The father saw that he must sell the house
That sheltered him, wherein his parents lived,
Round which his dearest memories clung in joy,
Where lived the partner of his life, where grew
From bud to blossom bright his children dear.
His wealth had gone in previous weddings spent,
And now if he forbore to sell his house
His dearest, youngest child must joyless be.
He told his wife about the sale to save
Themselves from sin, their child from grief.

The girl.
Did see unseen her parents' agony,

How they resolved to sacrifice themselves
For her sweet sake. A sudden tenderness
Flowed o' er her suffering soul in swelling tide
And bore her heart in prayer to Gouri's shrine.
She went with flying feet to where did shine
Her goddess bright and sought her help. A thought
Awoke in her and she resolved to die
That those who gave her life may live.
Also ! that this was so ! .

With radiant face
She went that day about her house, and did
Her daily work with absent looks, and heart
Laid at the holy feet of Gouri sweet.
Drest in her best she brought commingled joy
And grief to her belovéd parents' hearts.
With *Kunkum* spot upon her forehead bright
And prayers on her lips, she went about
Like Uma in her father's lofty home
By prayer and by penance and by vows
The love of Shiva seeking.

When night came
She found deliverance from her load of grief.
On her bright frame she placed devouring fire
And prayed that God might pure with saving flame
The souls of those who wrought her harm. She left
For her belovéd parents' solace poor
A letter with bright burning words that shine

As shone the flames that burnt her maiden frame
And left but ashes where a lovely soul
Had shone in lovely frame.

She wrote therein:.

"O mother sweet! O father dear! I die
To save you both from grief and ruin here.
My life I *owe* to you; I gladly give
It unto death that you may live. Our youths
Do speak of noble things but have no love
Or pity in their black and faithless hearts.
My mother Durga calls me to her heaven
And there in her sweet service shall I live
In joy for ever. Oh grieve not overmuch,
For we shall meet in joy by Durga's feet.
I die by fire: And let that fire that burns
My maiden frame spread o' er this holy land
And burn the plague-spots foul till she doth come
Out of her bath of fire with brighter limbs
And fierier soul to lead all sister lands
In love unto the lotus feet of God!
May this come true! O God! May this come true!

LIST OF ERRATA

Page.	Line.	For	Read.
2	24	given	giv'n
4	4	...	, (after fair)
4	6	...	, (after water)
14	18	,	.
14	23	This	The
16	4	agonised	agoniséd
21	3	cheerless	cheerful
22	3	after	afar
25	19	thee	thee,
28	5	wonderous	wondrous
29	6	beloved	belovéd
36	11	of	their
38	25	hands	hands,